INNOCENT VICTIMS

First published in the UK by Mia Campbell

A copy of the British Library Cataloguing in Publication Data is available from the British Library.

Paperback ISBN: 978-1-7394194-0-0
eBook ISBN: 978-1-7394194-1-7

Printed and bound in the UK

INNOCENT VICTIMS

Mia Campbell

Contents

Thumbprints in the Sandwiches

There were seven of us weans in that wee flat in Blackhill. For those who don't know, Blackhill is one of the most notorious areas of Glasgow, and even though our house has long been demolished, the area still has a reputation for its gangland culture, violence and poverty.

As a wean growing up, I wasn't really aware of just how dangerous the place was. Back then, I didn't know that my parents' favourite pub, the Provanmill Inn, was run by one of the UK's most notorious and feared gangsters, Arthur Thompson, who launched his 'career' as a money lender and would literally crucify people who couldn't pay their debts by nailing them to the floor or a door. Occasionally, my parents would come home from a drinking spree with black eyes, but Mum would never let on what had happened. She would just say they'd met some 'baddies'.

With seven weans and two parents in a three-bedroom flat, there were at least three of us in each bed every night and life was pretty chaotic. If we were lucky, we'd get custard for our dinner, and the closest we got to any physical attention was a steel comb through our hair to get rid of the nits. I remember being so hungry that I'd guddle about in the tin middens outside the closes to try to find something to eat.

Our parents were both heavy drinkers back then: Dad would raid the electric meter to get money for booze - QC fortified wine for him and Carlsberg Special for Mum - and they'd party away with the neighbours until the wee small hours, often having a shouting match just to round off the night.

I was the fourth in a family of four boys and three girls, born in Glasgow and named after the midwife who delivered me. My parents were Glaswegians through and through - think Rab C. Nesbitt and Mary Doll! - and although they were rubbish parents they were fundamentally decent people. Rough as it was, Blackhill was a fairly close-knit community, at least among the older residents, and visitors to the house would always be offered a wee cup of tea and a sandwich, even though the bread usually had a thumbprint in it or there was a bit of egg on the plate from the day before.

People looked out for each other in 70s Blackhill: one example of their neighbourliness was to warn others when the meter man was on his way, so that they could undo whatever jiggery-pokery they'd performed in order to avoid paying for leccy.

Mum was a Catholic and Dad was a Protestant - pretty unusual in those days - but Mum's mum refused to let them get married unless Dad changed his religion. He did. But he never let anyone forget it. "Fuck the Pope, ya Fenian bastards!" he'd yell out of the window, usually after a few fortified wines.

Every so often, Dad would get lifted for being drunk and disorderly and would spend the weekend at Her Majesty's Pleasure in Barlinnie. He always told us he'd fought in the Army, although that turned out not to be true. Although he had been in the Army when he was young, he never did any fighting as he'd been injured in an accident in Egypt, then he was hospitalised for three years, so ill with tuberculosis that it was feared he would never walk again.

Dad was as skinny as Mum was stout, although he was quite an attractive man who had an eye for the ladies. On one occasion, Mum went out searching for him, suspecting he might be at Mrs Findlay's down the road - and ignoring a nosey wifey who shouted at her that she should get back to her weans or she'd call the 'welfare'. Mrs Findlay came to the door looking flustered.

"Is Wullie here?" demanded Mum.

"Naw, hen, I huvnae seen him. He's no here".

Mum peered over Mrs Findlay's shoulder and could see wee plumes of smoke coming out of the wardrobe. Dad was attempting to hide but had forgotten to put his fag out.

Mum was one of three siblings and her sister Margaret is still alive and living in Blackhill. She's an odd sort, Margaret. I think she was bitter towards Mum because she had to stay and care for the old dear - my maternal grandmother - and so was denied the opportunity to get married and have children of her own.

When Mum had my brother Kenny, she was struggling to cope, so Margaret offered to take him in - and there he stayed, despite it supposedly only being for a wee while. One of my earliest memories is overhearing Margaret telling Mum that she wanted to take my wee bike for Kenny; I was about four or five at the time. "Well, take it while she's sleeping," I heard Mum say.

That night, I lay in bed with my sister Senga with the bike by my side and holding on to it like it was the Crown Jewels. Of course, I fell asleep eventually.

And in the morning, it had gone.

Glasgow from above, 1970s

Deprived area

Glasgow tenement building

Affordable housing

A Chaotic Childhood

Guddling around in middens and stealing oranges from the local shop became a way of life for me: I was always so hungry.

Our tea would consist of a piece and jam or dripping or maybe an egg sandwich or a plate of custard, eaten off saucers instead of proper plates. I realise now that we were malnourished, and it's little wonder I was such a sickly child, always pale and thin and in and out of hospital with bronchitis.

Mum would buy our clothes from the legendary Paddy's Market, founded more than two hundred years ago by Irish immigrants who sold their stuff to help pay for their ticket to America. When I was a wee girl, the market was a lifesaver for folk like us, but over the years it became associated with nefarious goings-on such as selling counterfeit goods and drug dealing, and was eventually closed down in 2009.

I don't really know why, but it became a tradition for Mum to buy us all a new outfit every first Sunday in May, but even so our shoes were either too big or too wee, and sometimes we had to go to school without any knickers on. I remember that once one of my sisters went to school wearing her nightie.

Life was tough and money was tight in 70s Blackhill, and to help the family finances I'd get sent round the neighbourhood selling Dad's LPs. One of my regular visits was to a house occupied by two young women, who befriended me and invited me in - only to chuck me into a freezing cold bath. I never told my parents though, as I didn't want to make any trouble.

So between that and raiding the meter, Mum and Dad managed to scrape together enough to get paralytic on QC fortified wine and Carlsberg Special.

With seven bairns and only three bedrooms, we just had to bunk up wherever we could. One morning I was slumbering on the sofa bed in the living-room when there was a knock at the door and, in her haste to answer it, Mum folded up the sofa bed with me still inside it. I tried calling out but nobody heard me at first, and several people actually sat down on me. Eventually, my sister heard my pathetic little voice and I was rescued. I guess with so many weans it's hard to keep track of them all.

I believe my mum and dad were good people; they just didn't know how to be parents. We had no rules, no boundaries, and no routine whatsoever.

We didn't have to make our beds; we just got up and went out the door, and we were never taught any life skills. Dad did all the cooking in our house - such as it was - although Mum could make a good pot of soup if she put her mind to it.

When I was nine, I picked up one of my parents' fags and smoked it quite openly. My sister Senga ran off to clipe on me, but all Dad said was "Aww, are you jealous? I'd raither she smoked in the hoose than go oot pickin' up dog ends."

So that was that. Though I knew some of the neighbours looked down on my parents for letting me smoke.

One day, a man chapped on the door asking if any of us bairns wanted to be on the telly. He may have been a real talent scout or he may just have been a chancer, although I know that there were a few documentaries made about Blackhill at the time. In fact, Mum and Dad had been asked if they wanted to appear, but they declined - although later we did see some of our neighbours on the telly. On that day, I remember Dad sending him away with a flea in his ear, saying "Not today, son." I never really forgave him for that, as the thought that I could have been famous rankled for years.

By then, we'd moved house so many times that people assumed we were gypsy travellers.

From Blackhill we moved to London Road in Bridgeton. We lived in a dark and dingy flat that Mum and Dad bought for about £50, and to reach it you had to go up one of those old- fashioned stone spiral staircases. It was my job to sweep the steps, and when I got to the bottom I'd brush all the dirt under the downstairs neighbour's doormat. Needless to say he wasn't best pleased, and I remember one day when Mum and Dad were coming in the front door he grabbed Mum by the throat because he thought she was the one sweeping the dirt under his mat. From there we moved to Easterhouse, another area of Glasgow known for its gang culture, although in its case the gangs were more territorial rather than involved with organised crime.. I remember very little about being in Easterhouse, apart from once again being bullied at school, and we weren't there long before we moved back to Blackhill - to the very same house we'd lived in before. Mum and Dad just couldn't settle: whenever there was trouble with the gangs or their debts caught up with them, Mum would say: "I dinnae like it here, I want tae move."

They'd built up debts on catalogues and HP - not massive amounts by today's standards, but more than they could afford. Sometimes they managed to dodge the debt collectors, but if one did manage to track them down, Mum would take to her bed, often staying there for weeks.

And if a debt collector turned up on the doorstep, we would get the blame.

"Are yer folks in?" they'd say.

"Aye, I'll just get them," we'd say innocently.

Dad never worked - at least, not until years later, and then only for a wee while - but had a modest Army pension, while Mum took occasional cleaning jobs in local shops and offices. One morning, when she and two friends were walking to work, they got run over by a car as they were crossing the road right outside St Philomena's Chapel. All three were injured and later were given compensation, although Mum's wasn't as much because she only had a broken leg, but still, every little helped. With seven weans, there just wasn't enough coming in to cover what they owed, so Dad would play on his health problems in order to get them on the priority housing list so they could run away from it all. Of course, all this flitting was unsettling for us kids, and for me, the fear of going to a new school - and meeting a fresh set of bullies - was almost overwhelming. That was why I started having conversations with God, begging Him to hurry up and make me a grown-up so that I didn't have to go through it any more.

Our playground

A burned-out home

Paddy's Market, where Mum used to take us

Gangland Glasgow

One of our neighbours in Blackhill was Paul Ferris, an enforcer for the 'Godfather', Arthur Thompson, and one of Scotland's most infamous criminals.

In his role as a debt collector for Thompson, Ferris would stab, blind or knee-cap anyone who defaulted on their payments, and was feared throughout the neighbourhood - and beyond - for his brutality.

As my parents used to drink in the Provanmill Inn, then owned by Thompson and from where he ran his criminal empire, they had several encounters with the gangsters of the time, on one occasion being forced to hide a quantity of stolen jewellery in their house. The stash included gold and diamonds, and although they were petrified, they couldn't say no for fear of the consequences.

Fortunately they were tipped off that the polis were coming to raid their house - so in a blind panic, my mum and sister quickly put on all the rings and necklaces. When the polis turned up, they didn't find anything. To be honest, they obviously weren't very bright, as there can't have been many Blackhill women who accessorised their peenies with expensive jewellery.

So thankfully they got away with it and avoided getting into trouble with the law as well as a beating - or worse - from the gangsters who'd coerced them.

Back in the 70s and 80s, the likes of Thompson and Ferris were universally feared.

Thompson had begun his underworld career as a money

lender before moving into protection rackets, bank robberies and heists. It was rumoured that, by the 90s, he was earning around £100,000 a week as a loan shark. He then invested his ill-gotten gains into legitimate businesses, which made him incredibly wealthy, and he lived in a big house in Provanmill that he called The Ponderosa after the ranch in the TV series *Bonanza*.

Gang rivalry in Glasgow was brutal back then and God help anyone who got caught in the middle of a 'disagreement'. In the 60s, Thompson was charged with murder when he killed two members of the Welsh family gang in Blackhill - but he couldn't be prosecuted as no-one was prepared to testify against him, even though the offence happened on a busy road in front of a number of witnesses.

Thompson had forced the men's van off the road and into a lamppost, killing them both, in an act of revenge for the bomb he believed they'd planted under his car, causing an explosion that killed his mother-in-law. A couple of years later, his wife Rita forced her way into the Welsh home and stabbed the widow of Patrick Welsh in the chest. She was jailed for three years.

Thompson died of a heart attack in 1993 at the age of 61, but even today his grandchildren and great grandchildren have to remain anonymous for the safety of the family.

Two years before Thompson died, his son, Arthur Jr., who was by then in charge of the family drug trade, was shot dead - and Thompson's former partner-in-crime, Paul Ferris, was charged with his murder. After what was then the longest trial in Scottish criminal history, he was found not guilty.

However, having already served several sentences for various offences, he was imprisoned again from 1998 to 2002 for trading in firearms and possessing explosives.

While behind bars he wrote his first book about his criminal activities and one of them, *The Wee Man,* was made into a film starring Martin Compston. Today, he's an acknowledged author and business consultant living in London.

The Best Days of Your Life?

I hated school from the moment I started until I left at fifteen with not a single qualification to my name. Every day I'd have knots in my stomach because I knew I was going to get battered. Walking to school was like running the gauntlet of gangsters; they'd shout at you, pull you down by the hair onto the pavement and give you a good kicking - and that was just at primary.

At St Philomena's in Blackhill, I was bullied constantly, and I never really knew why. I was a sickly child and a loner, so maybe it was because of that. Or maybe it was because of the way I looked. We were just packed off every morning without any breakfast and wearing any scabby old clothes we could find; I think the teachers felt sorry for us, because they'd take off our tops and give us all a sloppy Joe sweatshirt to wear for the day. I don't know if they thought we'd be warmer, or whether it was because our own clothes were so minging. Even in the classroom no-one wanted to come near me, and I dreaded the 'tag' game, whereby we had to stand with our arms folded and the teacher would whisper in another child's ear the name of the child they had to tag. It was meant to be a wee tap on the shoulder, but I always got thumped so hard that it brought tears to my eyes. I'd go home bruised and humiliated, my only comfort being the conversations I believed I was having with God.

At other times, I'd seek escape by playing on the parked-up trains in the sidings at Central Station , or jumping in and out of the lifts in the high-rise flats or at the Royal Infirmary, where I was treated for bronchitis.

As St Philomena's was a Catholic school, going to Confession was mandatory. In my desperation to be accepted, I'd buy sweets and single cigarettes to bribe my classmates, using money I stole from my mum. Fearing I'd go to the burning fire, I went to Confession one day to own up to having taken ten shillings (a lot of money then, but about 50p in today's values) in a pathetic attempt to try to buy the other kids' friendship and stop the daily batterings. The priest, as usual, was lurking unseen behind a screen, but there was a picture of Jesus opposite and I decided to appeal directly to Him rather than go through the middleman. Unfortunately, I'd forgotten to close the door behind me, so the entire class - including the teacher - had ringside seats to my confession. The priest gave me twenty Hail Marys; my classmates had a good laugh and I learned a valuable lesson.

It wasn't long before we were on the move again, and I was enrolled in Whitburn Academy, where once again I was bullied mercilessly for no reason that I could fathom. In fact, at least in Whitburn my clothes were better, as my friend's mum would sell clothes to my mum and let her pay them up. If I was lucky, there'd be a few Bay City Rollers items in there, so I'd strut about in my tartan gear thinking I was the bees' knees.

When Senga wasn't around, I'd meet up with her friend Janice, who sometimes took me to her favourite 'haunt' - one in a row of council-owned garages, which had lost its door and so made a perfect place to hang out. Janice had a younger brother, Jimmy, and he and I embarked on a wee romance that involved little more than a bit of snogging - but that came to an end when he sent me home one day with a huge love bite and I got a right battering from Mum and Dad. On top of that, the council got the garage door sorted, putting a stop to any further winching.

When I wasn't dogging school - dogging had a different meaning back then - I made friends with a girl called Lily, and she and I became partners in crime.

She had an adult friend in Armadale, and we'd often hitch a lift or walk to her house, helping her out with her five weans, doing a bit of housework and going to the shops for her. This went on for about a year, occasionally being interrupted by a visit from the truant officer. We did go to school from time to time, but even when we didn't I'd lie through my teeth, swearing blind that I'd been there but had just missed registration.

Around the same time, Lily and I became obsessed with two local boys, Asif and Hammy. With his dark complexion, brown eyes and black curly hair, Asif was the one I fancied, while Lily went for Hammy, who was taller and paler. The only problem was that we were too shy to approach them, so pretty much ended up as a couple of stalkers; the guys obviously noticed, as one day they stopped and let us catch up with them. Just as it had been with Jimmy, the romance with Asif was no more than a bit of snogging - at least to start with. But then one day he got carried away and 'slipped the hand' on me; I was horrified, and whatever candle I held for him was snuffed in an instant.

Like many Scottish communities, Whitburn had an annual gala day, which started with a traditional parade and often ended in carnage as the locals spilled out of the pubs. While the adults got stocious, us weans would spend the day at the shows, riding on the rollercoaster, big wheel, and waltzers until we ran out of dosh. Looking back, Whitburn had been a positive move in many ways - we had better clothes, nicer pals, relatively sober parents, and an altogether less scary environment.

Skiving school became a way of life for me. I'd climb out of the bedroom window, shimmy down the drainpipe, and just take off, mooching about for the day and conversing with God until it was time to go home again. One time before I went out, I put one of those plastic doll's heads on my pillow - the ones with hair that wee girls used to comb - and when my dad finally came to 'wake me up' it rolled onto the floor, almost giving him a heart attack.

To avoid lessons, I'd either hide in the toilets or just hang about the streets smoking the fags I'd stolen from my mum. One day when I was about thirteen, I nicked some money from her purse and a friend and I got a bus into Glasgow city centre, where we shamelessly approached complete strangers and asked them for cash, telling them that we'd lost our bus fare. Some people actually did give us money, but there was one man who, instead of giving us the cash, offered us somewhere to stay for the evening. In our naivety, we accepted his offer and followed him to what we assumed would be his flat. Instead, we were led into a totally bare room right at the top of a high-rise block. The next thing I remember is seeing my pal lying on her jacket in a corner of the hard concrete floor and calling out for her, but she didn't respond. Then the guy laid me down and wrapped his arms and legs around me; I was terrified.

"I'm really feart," I sobbed. "I want to go hame!"

"Shut it!", he shouted, clamping his hand over my mouth.

That's all I can remember of that evening, but in the morning neither of us felt right. Thankfully the guy had gone, so we got a bus home, where we found a welcoming party in the form of the local polis. They asked us where we'd been and of course, we lied and told them we'd just been wandering the streets. I got a right battering for running away, and I never did it again.

Eventually my skiving got so bad that I had to appear before a Children's Hearing. For anyone unfamiliar with the Children's Panel, it's a system of juvenile justice unique to Scotland, whereby trained volunteers make decisions about children who find themselves in trouble for a variety of reasons - including non-attendance at school. The decisions Panel members make are legally binding, so to say I was scared that day is an understatement. The girl who appeared before me came out of the hearing room in floods of tears; she'd been sent to a residential school and I was terrified I was going to suffer the same fate. My dad came with me to the hearing and I could see by his face how worried he was that I was going to be sent away. He was almost greetin' as he pleaded with the Panel members to let me stay at home, telling them I was too poorly to be sent to residential.

So I went to a special school, Polkemmet, near Whitburn, where we were taught in huts by a lovely teacher who made me feel safe and secure at last. She was kind and patient with me and, as it was a much smaller class than I'd had to cope with before, I felt much more relaxed, especially since we were taught basic, primary lessons and I wasn't so feart about having to answer a question in front of the others.

My younger brother Duncan was in one of the other huts as he had learning difficulties and was a troubled wee soul - and to be honest, he still is. When I was nine and he was seven, we'd both been sexually abused by one of our parents' drinking pals, which I talk about later in the book.

Having dogged school so much, my record was so poor that I remember scoring nothing out of a hundred in a test, so leaving was pretty much the only option.

I left school in May of that year, turned sixteen in June, and was married in July.

Having a rare day out, when I was about 7 years old

Myself on the day of my Holy Communion

Back yard of a tenement with washing lines and middens

Seven Years

The move to Whitburn was a positive one for for my parents, as they were older by then and away from the party lifestyle they'd had back in Blackhill, so the QC and Carlsberg Special didn't have the same appeal. We lived in two different houses in Whitburn before moving to Livingston, first to Deans and then to Addiewell.

It was while we were in Addiewell hat I met Derek. I was introduced to him by a pal, who was going out with his brother, Johnny. I'm not quite sure what happened to the pal as one minute she was there and the next she'd gone; I'm pretty sure she must have been taken into care. Anyway, Johnny and I ended up together; he was a real gentleman, always walking me home at night and restricting any physical activity to a kiss and a cuddle as he said he respected me too much to try anything else. He was generous too, on one occasion giving me £70 to buy some new clothes at Ingliston market. I truly loved that boy, so I was absolutely heartbroken when he said he was going to England to find work. He promised he'd come back for me, but Mum was dubious.

"He's no interested in you," she said.

But I was only fifteen and in love, or so I thought. I yearned for the day he'd return. And a few months later, return he did - with his pregnant girlfriend in tow. It was the same girl who'd introduced us, so they'd obviously hooked up again while I sat at home pining for him.

So that's how I ended up with Derek.

He was tall, dark, and handsome; our relationship

developed quickly, and even though I hadn't even reached the age of sixteen, we decided to get married. My teacher told me it was madness to get engaged at fifteen, and of course, she was right.

I knew absolutely nothing about sex and even though I was about to get married I still hadn't started my periods; Mum and Dad just didn't talk about any of that stuff, although I knew roughly what to expect from talking to girls at school.

I started my periods on the day I ordered my wedding cake. Derek and I were staying at Mum and Dad's, sleeping in bunk beds. Me in the top one, him at the bottom. In the morning, I woke up to find my sheets saturated with blood, and at the same time, I kind of knew but didn't know what had happened.

I was so embarrassed that I knew I couldn't tell my parents, so I got Derek to burn the sheets in the fireplace - thank goodness we still had coal fires back then - but I remember my dad shouting: "What the fuck is that burning?" But there was no way I could let on to my parents, just as I hadn't been able to tell them about the shooting pains I'd had the week before. I just suffered in silence. Of course, I later realised that the pain was my body adjusting to womanhood, but I don't think I've ever got over the emotional changes I went through - indeed, I believe that was to mark the start of my lifelong struggle with my mental health.

As I didn't have any money, I had to use cut-up rags for protection, but luckily the whole horrible business was over with by the time I got married two weeks later. It was a low-key ceremony in a registry office in West Calder and I didn't really know what I was doing: I was like a wee girl playing grown-ups. I wore an old-fashioned white wedding dress with long sleeves and a hood that Mum had bought for £11 from a woman she knew, and the whole fiasco was followed by a meal in a hotel to the accompaniment of one man and his accordion. And he was no Jimmy Shand, I can tell you.

About a week later, I decided I didn't like being married and wanted to go home to Mum and Dad, so I got on a bus to their house.

"You've made yer bed, now lie in it!" they said. "Now get yersel back hame."

I was so young when I married Derek that I didn't know how to cope. We were given a council house, but we couldn't afford a cooker, so he made meals on a camping stove. We were so hard-up that we'd walk the six miles to my parents' house to borrow money for food, and rummaged about in skips to see if there was anything we could use.

Derek's older sister lived in Sussex, so we sold all our belongings and spent a few months with her in the hope that he could find a job. When that plan failed we returned to Scotland, and lived with my parents for a while until we were allocated a one-bedroom house in Livingston. After we'd been together for two years, I discovered I was pregnant. Still only eighteen, I was naive to the ways of the world and I can feel a blush coming on as I tell the story of my first examination.

"Take your clothes off and come through," said the nurse. So I did. All of them. How was I to know I was supposed to leave my underwear on? To compound my embarrassment, the doctor was young and rather good-looking.

I gave birth to Mandy in Bangour Hospital, missing the latest episode of *Crossroads* in the process. I was still so young and found the whole business so traumatic that I swore I'd never do it again, although I guess all first-time mums say that while they're in the throes of labour.

Mandy was a healthy weight - 7lb 6oz - but as I hadn't delivered the placenta I needed an operation. Never having had any surgery before, I was so scared that I refused to begin with, not realising I could be risking my life. But Mum and Dad knew how important it was to go through with it, so promised me an extra large Easter egg as a bribe. I went through with it, but I'm still waiting for that bastard Easter egg.

I was in hospital for seven days after that, but got no support from the other mums.

"Look at that wean having a wean!" they'd say. "Aye, she should be ashamed of hersel'"

Derek did all the cooking, cleaning, and everything else, and not long after Mandy was born my mental health had deteriorated to the point that I became agoraphobic.

Little by little, our marriage crumbled, and I knew that I wasn't capable of caring for my daughter, so I left her with her dad. I tried so hard to visit her, but some days I just couldn't do it, and it broke my heart to think of her wee face at the window looking out for a mum who hardly ever came. If I tried to go out, I'd have panic attacks so severe that I thought I would die; I just didn't understand what was happening to me. I rarely left the house, although occasionally I'd venture out to see my mum. But once there, I'd stand behind the couch for the whole visit. "Come and sit doon", she'd say. "I cannae, I cannae," I'd say. "I need to get back down the road."

The marriage lasted for seven years and Mandy was cared for all that time by her dad. The same week as I started to write this book, Derek died of cancer, and it hit Mandy hard. She has her own mental health issues that have been exacerbated by her grief.

Derek and I had a good relationship after our marriage ended and Mandy and I cared for him in his final days. Towards the end, I told him that it wasn't his fault that we broke up and thanked him for doing such a great job in bringing up our daughter. RIP Derek.

Myself aged 15 with one of my Nephews

Myself and my daughter Mandy

My daughter Mandy and her father Derek

My Lost Child

After my marriage to Derek ended, I moved into a bedsit with a pal, and began to feel better. I even got a job as a cleaner, which boosted my confidence no end.

And it was around that time that I met Dougie, the guy who'd found the bedsit for us. He was without doubt the most charismatic man I've ever known, and when he roared up on his motorbike with his long dreadlocks streaming out behind him, I felt like a love-struck teenager. I was so smitten that I blanked out the warning signs of what lay ahead.

We'd only been going out for a few weeks when Dougie's sister, Maureen, came round along with one of his pals. From the outset, Dougie was a heavy drinker, and this particular evening, after a few swallies, he pushed me onto the floor and started banging my head on the carpet. Trying hard not to cry, I told myself he was just playing.

"That wasnae playing,", said his pal.

All the same, I was so besotted that I dismissed the incident; I felt that God had given me a second chance in life when he came along.

Another time, I'd just come out of the bath, wearing just a towel, when a load of guys from the other flats turned up, wanting to fiddle the meter so they could get free electricity for one of the rooms. I felt so intimidated that I thought I was going to be gang-raped.

"I can't stay here", I sobbed.

"Well, move in with me then," said Dougie. So I did.

Big mistake.

I tried so hard to please him, cleaning the place and trying to make it homely. But as it only had one bedroom I struggled to find anywhere to store stuff, so I put some shoes in a unit in the lounge. Fuelled by booze, as usual, he picked up a shoe and threw it at me. That was just the start of a catalogue of violence that became even worse after the birth of our son, Andrew, two years later.

Dougie would lift the wee man out of his high chair and, while holding him, would put the boot into me, leaving me bruised and battered. To this day, I still have a dent in my head where he threw an ashtray at me. On one occasion, when I was lying on the bed, he pulled the massive TV off the wall and threw it at me. When my eyes were too black to take Andrew to nursery, Dougie would take him so no-one could see, always full of remorse for the injuries he'd inflicted on me.

"I'm sorry, I'm sorry, I didnae mean it," he'd say.

Dougie was an intelligent man who once had dreams of being a teacher, but the booze got the better of him - and I didn't help, it has to be said. I'd go across the road to the shop for him and buy a crate of beer and half a bottle of vodka, unaware of the damage I was doing, but at the same time worried about the consequences if I didn't comply.

Often, he'd say he was going to work, but would spend the day in the pub, and I knew I'd be in for a battering when he eventually rolled in.

To my dismay, when Andrew was only around nine months old I discovered I was pregnant again. I really didn't want another baby, but I didn't want a termination either, and neither did Dougie.

"It's murder!", he said, then added: "But my sister cannae have a family".

What the hell did that mean?

I was about to find out, as before I knew it he was down at his mum's telling her that I was having a baby for Maureen. I was distraught. Much as I didn't want another child, I knew I couldn't give my baby away. I even visited my local priest to ask for guidance: he told me that as long as I knew that the bairn was being properly cared for, then God wouldn't judge me for giving up my baby. His words were of little comfort, as I knew I'd rather have a termination than give up my child.

By that time, I was twenty-nine years old, but very timid and withdrawn. My friend Wilma told me I was making a big mistake in allowing my baby to go to Maureen, and I knew she was right - but I felt powerless to stop it happening. I remember Dougie dragging me across the bathroom floor by my hair, yelling: "If you do anything to hurt my sister, I'll kill you and I'll take Andrew and you'll never see that bairn again!"

I felt so used, so scared. I began to really resent Dougie, but had nowhere to go. Cruel as he was, I couldn't believe that he was capable of giving our child away. In the run-up to the birth, he and his sister told me a pack of lies, presumably in the hope of bringing me round. Maureen and her husband Jim told me they were going to move to a house just along the road from Dougie and me, and that I'd be a part of my child's life. They even told me I'd be known as 'Mummy number two.'

Maureen was at the bottom of the bed when my daughter Kirsten was born, and visited us every day for the eight days we were in hospital. I could tell that the nurses had an idea something was up, but I was too afraid to say anything. On day eight, Dougie, his mum, Maureen and her husband turned up to collect me and took me back to his mum's house, where

I was made to hand over the baby. The pain I felt that day is indescribable. It was as if my baby had died, and I never recovered - nor did I ever forgive Dougie. I saw Kirsten a couple of times as a baby, and one day I was horrified to see a breast pump lying on the sofa. It was obscene; how could she possibly breastfeed my child?

I begged Maureen to give me my baby back, but my pleas fell on deaf ears and her attitude changed. No longer was she the kindly foster mum allowing visitation rights; they moved to Aberdeenshire and contact was lost. The only photos I have of my daughter are the ones Andrew managed to steal, but even as a wee boy he knew what he was doing was risky. "Dinnae say anything, Mum," he'd say. "Otherwise I'd be in deep crap."

I was tortured: everywhere I went I looked for her, hoping against hope that I'd recognise her and we'd be reconciled.

I was in Savacentre in Edinburgh one day when I spotted Maureen, her mum, and Kirsten, who by then was about five years old. I'd have known her anywhere; she was my child, after all. As I got closer, I heard Maureen tell her mum: "Take Kirsten to the toilet!" Her mum scurried away with my wee girl, obviously not wanting me to see her, but at that point - to my eternal regret - I lost the plot.

I leaned across the chilled cabinet, grabbed Maureen by the hair and screamed: "How can a human being do what you did to another human being?!" I know I shouldn't have done it, but my emotions were out of control. From the day my daughter was taken away from me, I had been consumed with bitterness, sadness, and regret. I just wanted my baby back. Kirsten had been whisked away by her 'granny', so she wouldn't have witnessed the scene, but years later it was to come back to haunt me.

When I met my dear friend Gary, who's now my carer and a tower of strength, we went together to a solicitor, who told us that after two years had gone by Maureen was entitled to adopt Kirsten. By then, more than two years had passed and my wee girl had been adopted, so we hadn't a leg to stand on. The only hope I had of seeing my daughter was to ask for some kind of contact. The letter from Maureen's solicitor in response to my request read: 'Over her dead body.'

Kirsten would be thirty years old now, and I grieve for her still. I last saw her about eight years ago, when Andrew said she'd been in touch and wanted to meet up with us both. I was full of excitement and anticipation as I headed to Edinburgh; I couldn't believe that we were to be reconciled after all these years. For Andrew, I took a watch that had been given to me by my mother, and for Kirsten I took a gold necklace engraved with the words: 'Even though time stands still, we're always together.'

Kirsten, Maureen and Jim; Andrew, Gary and I all met in Princes Street. Kirsten was the spitting image of her brother, although she had always referred to him as 'a distant cousin', which broke his heart. It was with trembling hands that I gave her the necklace - and almost immediately, she threw it in the nearest bin.

She asked me if I thought it was okay for me to attack Maureen - an attack she couldn't possibly have known about unless she was told, and even then I daresay the scene had been embellished. I told her no, I knew it wasn't right, but that my emotions had got the better of me. The next thing she said shocked me to the very core.

"I brought you here to tell you how much I hate you," she spat.

"I can't wait to get telt that you've died so I can jump up and down on your coffin. Do you understand me? If you ever see me, you cross over to the other side of the road. Do I make myself clear?"

This was my daughter, the person I'd given birth to, the person I'd been forced to give up. God knows what she'd been told over the years, how much her mind had been poisoned.

I'd been gearing myself up for years for this meeting; I'd been hoping and praying that we'd be reconciled and that we could have a mother and daughter relationship at last. I was devastated by her viciousness, made so much worse by her startling resemblance to Andrew.

"I'm alright, I'm alright," I told Gary, before collapsing in the street with shock and grief.

I just couldn't get the scene out of my mind; I was haunted by the fact that my own daughter appeared to want me dead.

The torment in my head was so unbearable that there was only one way I felt I could find peace.

So, a couple of weeks later I was driving along the Abington Road in South Lanarkshire when something in me snapped. Seeing a bend up ahead, I put my foot on the accelerator as hard as I could, spinning out of control and landing upside down on the verge. My hair was stuck to the roof of the car and blood was pouring down my face, but my attempt at taking my own life had failed.

I didn't know what to feel at that point; I don't know whether I was disappointed or glad to be alive. After a few minutes, I managed to scramble out of the car window and stop a passing motorist. "I've had a wee accident", I said simply.

The driver took me to the hospital, where I spent such an uncomfortable night that I begged the staff to let me go home. The next day they discharged me, my forehead grotesquely swollen and my body aching so much that I could barely move. Having to get up to use the bathroom was sheer agony.

The physical pain was bad enough, but the emotional pain was so much worse. I just couldn't believe that this young woman, the daughter I gave birth to, could be so cruel. She may not like it, but at the end of the day she's part of me, and I would meet her again if I could. That episode of my life will stay with me forever; I'll take the sadness I feel to my grave.

I know now that she's a married woman with children - my grandchildren. I can't change what happened and I try hard not to dwell on it, but if she by chance softened and wanted to meet, I'd be there.

Shortly before Dougie died four years ago, aged just fifty- five, Kirsten told him she forgave him for what he'd done. Once again, my emotions were thrown into turmoil. How could she? How could she ever forgive a man who almost literally wrenched a child away from its own mother?

Although we never married, Dougie and I were together - on and off - for nine years. Towards the end, the irresistible, charismatic man I'd known was reduced to nothing more than a skeleton as his body was ravaged by skin cancer, and his death hit me hard.

He was an alcoholic. He beat me black and blue. He stole my child.

The Demon Drink

I was fifteen when I had my first proper experience with alcohol. I'd not long met Derek when we went out with his sister to the Murray Bar in West Calder, even though I was underage. His sister asked me what I wanted to drink, and of course, I hadn't a clue, so I asked what Derek was having. She told me he was on the rum, so I said I'd have the same. Then she asked what I wanted in it - again, I had no idea, so I naively said 'nothing', and just drank it neat. I wasn't much more than a child, and this was all new to me, so I didn't realise it had to be diluted. Oh my God, I've never been so ill in all my life, and for years I wouldn't have any more than a wee glass of sherry.

Alcohol was almost literally in the family's blood. My parents were heavy drinkers, at least until they moved away from Blackhill; Dad's sister was a very heavy drinker and her two children, my cousins, became heavy drinkers too. In fact, one of them died aged forty-five from alcohol poisoning, and before she passed her friends even took booze into the hospital for her.

After my experience with the undiluted rum, I hardly touched a drop for years. But Dougie was an alcoholic, and over time I started to join him in having a drink, enjoying the buzz it gave me. I remember saying to him: "I feel I needed that."

Perhaps surprisingly, he tried to discourage me, saying: "That's it, you're no gettin' any mair."

Although my level of drinking was nowhere near his - I

was getting through about a quarter of a bottle each night - deep down I knew it was helping to block things out. It helped me cope with the violence he subjected me to and the depression that has dogged me for all my life.

That quarter-bottle became a whole bottle of vodka every night and I'd plead with Mandy to get me more before the local shop closed. I was desperately seeking oblivion, and found it at the bottom of a bottle of Smirnoff, or the own-brand equivalent. Or whatever happened to be on the shelf. By then, my drinking was so out of control that I even sold my gold jewellery to get the money for vodka.

Even though she had her own troubles, my daughter Mandy was so worried about me - and the impact my drinking could have on her three young children - that she booked me into hospital, where I was weaned off the stuff with large doses of vitamin B12. It was initially intended to be a five-day stay, but I ended up there for thirteen days. The first thing that happened was that I was given medication that made me feel as though I was drunk, then after a couple of nights I took a seizure - a common effect of alcohol withdrawal. We were also offered talking therapy, which was a disaster. I was so nervous in a group setting that I'd burst into hysterical laughter at even the saddest of stories, and was totally incapable of controlling myself.

I'll never know for sure, but I may have paid an enormous price for my heavy drinking. A brain scan has revealed cognitive impairment, which doctors say could be a symptom of Korsakoff 's Syndrome, a form of dementia most commonly caused by excessive use of alcohol - or it could have been caused by the injury to my head in my pathetic attempt at suicide.

I've also been left with peripheral neuropathy, a nervous disorder that gets worse if I do have a drink. I wake up next day not being able to feel my hands or feet.

The bevvy was one thing, but drugs were out of the question for me - illegal ones anyway. With my complex mental health issues, I have relied on prescription medication for years and, at one time, when I was with Dougie, I was even prescribed purple hearts. I'd be sitting in a chair, too depressed to even move, and he'd open my mouth, hold my nose, and throw the tablets down my throat as if I was a cat or a dog. It wouldn't take long before I was up, buzzing about and hurtling around the house like a dervish, cleaning everything in sight.

When I was drunk, I'd sometimes phone my mum, telling her the secret I'd kept to myself for years.

"You dinnae know the real truth," I'd say to her. "Dad's pal abused me when I was wee."

"Dinnae be so daft", she'd say. "Yer dad would never have allowed it."

Deep down, though, I think she must have known.

This is what happens when I get carried away

Myself and Les McKeown at his book signing

The demon drink

Innocent Victims

I was nine and Duncan was seven when we were abused by one of Dad's drinking pals, a man who lived a couple of closes along from us in Blackhill. It happened at separate times and neither of us knew until later what the other was going through.

I have only the vaguest memories of the perpetrator - fawn trousers and a fawn top with black stripes - but I remember his dad very well, as he was a dead ringer for Frank Cannon, a TV detective in the seventies. Everybody said so. I don't know if he knew what his son was up to, but I remember being called across and told to go up to the flat.

There was a table that lay lengthways in front of the lounge window, and he would draw the curtains before lifting me on to it. Then he'd pull down my pants and his trousers and show me his 'thing'. I have memories of seeing blood on it, but don't know how it got there; as far as I know he didn't drug me or ply me with alcohol, but I believe I must have passed out and blocked out whatever happened to me. It's a distinct possibility that he raped me, although I couldn't say for sure - but later, much later, after I'd had Mandy, I was told my chances of having more children were slim because there were signs of internal damage.

After such an ordeal, you may wonder why I kept going back. Well, the truth is that I was too terrified not to.

"If you say anything to your dad, I'm going to tell him you've been dirty", he said.

So all the while I kept my mouth shut, and the abuse

continued until we moved out of Blackhill. The school knew about it and the hospital knew about it too, but nothing was done. Thank God things are different today.

When, years later, I told Mum what had happened, she was so upset that I changed my story.

"It didnae really happen, Mum," I told her. "I just said that because I was pissed. It was just the drink talking. Nothing happened."

At the same time as I was being abused, my poor wee brother Duncan was suffering in his own private hell. Not only was the same neighbour violating him in the kitchen, he was also being abused by a guy across the road, which I saw with my own eyes.

I remember the guy didn't live in that close but was always there, the man in black. He'd sit on the step of the house across the street, pull Duncan's trousers down and hold him in his arms like a baby.

When I told my mum, she just said: "Tell him to come hame."

Poor Duncan had some really tough times as a child, and has struggled ever since, even trying to take his own life when he was still a young lad. In those days, he and his pals would play 'hudgin the buses', whereby they'd get a free ride by clinging to the metal poles on the platform at the back of the bus. But one day one of his mates lost his grip, fell into the path of a taxi, and was killed.

Heartbroken by the loss of his friend and tortured by the memories of abuse, Duncan tried to do exactly the same thing, but fell on to the pavement and, apart from a few bruises, was unhurt.

3 of my Brothers playing outside the shops in Blackhill,
in the early 1970's

Hogganfield Street in Blackhill,
where I was brought up as a young child

A typical tenement close

Picking Up the Pieces

I was forty-five years old when I first told my mother I loved her. Ach, you're only saying that cos you've got a drink in you", she said.

"Tell me again tomorrow when you're sober."

After that, I told her every time I phoned her, and I'm pleased to say the rest of the family started saying it too. She hadn't been the best mum in the world, but she was our mum, and it wasn't her fault she didn't know how to be a proper parent. Her own mother, my granny, was a right battle-axe who didn't hide her dislike of me by calling me names and slapping me, always reducing me to tears. She was your archetypal wee Glasgow wifey, with a skirt just past her knees, a wee green cardigan, ankle boots, and a peeny permanently tied round her waist.

I don't really know why she hated me so much. Maybe it was just because I was my mother's daughter, as she definitely favoured my Auntie Margaret over my mum, or maybe it was because she was a bitter old woman. Her husband had walked out on her one day and had never come back, so I never knew my maternal grandfather.

Mum was one of three; her brother Ian was a pretty decent boxer in his youth and in fact had once punched Arthur Thompson, who was later to become the feared gangster who brought terror to Glasgow.

I really liked my Uncle Ian; he never married but had a string of increasingly gorgeous girlfriends and I loved going to chapel with him and whoever was on his arm at the time.

It broke my heart to see how cruelly he was treated by his sister Margaret and my brother Kenny. Now, Ian is buried alongside my mum in Tillicoultry, and my dad's ashes are scattered alongside them.

As I write, Margaret is still alive and well into her eighties.

As a child, I remember her green leather coat that she always wore with black, knee-high boots, and her face like a smacked arse. She was bitter that she was the one who had to care for the old granny and that marriage and motherhood passed her by. She had taken Kenny in from birth and she was going to have me too, but I wasn't well enough for her liking: I was in and out of hospital with bronchitis and I remember I had a sore ear when she didn't want me after all.

I don't think I'll ever forgive Margaret for stealing my precious tricycle that night. I remember it so well, with its bright red frame and white seat, and I cried buckets after it disappeared. To add insult to injury, she turned up one day with a Polaroid photo of Kenny sitting on the trike wearing full cowboy regalia, brandishing a silver cap gun. What a thieving witch.

And that wasn't the only time she stole from me. One day when the bell had gone at St Philomena's, the teacher asked me to stay behind for a bit. I was about seven years old, timid and feart. I had no idea what was going on or what I'd done wrong. So I meekly followed the teacher along the corridor, secretly enjoying the clickety-clack sound her shoes made on the floor. She took me into a room where there was another woman waiting, holding the biggest, prettiest doll I'd ever seen, with golden ringlets cascading down her back.

"This is for you", she said simply. There was no explanation, but I can only assume that she'd heard about our family's circumstances and was being charitable.

I raced home clutching the doll, which I christened Cinderella, and excitedly showed it to the family, which that day included Auntie Margaret. Cinderella was my pride and joy; I played with her constantly, brushing her beautiful hair and talking to her like she was my best pal. Every day after school, the first thing I did was run to her. I'd only had Cinderella for about a week when one day when I came home from school and couldn't find her. I was frantic, but instinctively knew where she'd gone. I was heartbroken.

I feel sorry for all my siblings - except perhaps Senga, of which more later - but my heart really goes out to Kenny, who's had his mind poisoned for years. After he was sent to stay with Margaret, Mum went on to have another son, Malkie, so I can only imagine the sense of abandonment Kenny felt at being the only one of seven weans to be excluded from his family, especially after we upped sticks from Glasgow and moved to West Lothian. And especially after being told by your aunt that your mother didn't want you.

When I told Auntie Margaret that Kenny was being bullied at school, she accused me of being a liar, so I didn't bother contacting her again, although I knew only too well what he was going through. Mum tried everything to please her, but if she said something she didn't like, she'd go into a major huff and not speak to Mum for weeks.

At one stage in his life, Kenny began sniffing glue as a way of coping, but thankfully didn't progress to anything harder - thanks mainly to Mum and Dad, who went through to Glasgow to help him. Considering they'd pretty much given him up when he was wee, that seems just a tad ironic, but deep down they cared for all of us and I believe they always regretted what they'd done.

We learned quite recently that Auntie Margaret plans to

leave all her money to Edinburgh Dog and Cat Home, but we'll do everything in our power to get justice for Kenny and make sure that he gets what he deserves after the miserable life he had with her.

To this day, Kenny lives in Glasgow, and I speak to him as often as I can. He's lonely and troubled, haunted by the memories of his childhood and, to add to his heartache, his non-verbal autistic teenage daughter has been taken away from him. He begged one of us to care for her instead, but how could we? It would be far too much of a challenge.

My eldest brother, Ally, is a heavy drinker and Malkie, the youngest, suffers from anxiety, so we all struggle in one way or another as a result of our past. Ally, Malkie, Duncan and I often talk on the phone, which helps us come to terms with our childhood - the bullying, the hunger, the boozing. Apart from Pauline, the eldest, who now works as a counsellor, all my siblings have struggled throughout their lives to come to terms with our dysfunctional childhood.

Of all the bairns, I like to think I was the favourite, but perhaps that's just wishful thinking.

I was always joking around and making my mum laugh, singing and dancing and having a right carry-on. Even as an adult, I'd go round to Mum's and she'd say: "Let's see what we can find for you", and I'd leave with a bag full of 'treasures'. I only needed to admire something in the house and Mum would give it to me. This didn't go down at all well with my sister Senga, who made it plain that she was jealous.

Senga is two years older than me and, like Mum and her sister, she'd blow hot and cold. Sometimes she'd speak to me and sometimes she wouldn't; I remember when I visited Mum she'd make a cup of tea for everyone but me.

She hasn't spoken to me since we were teenagers; she claims that when I was thirteen I stole some clothes of hers, which may or may not be true - I can't remember - but that seems to be a daft reason to hold a grudge for nearly fifty years. Still, that's Senga for you - always in the huff for one reason or another, just like her Auntie Margaret. While I was being abused by the man in Blackhill, I was convinced that she was too, as I used to see her going into his house and the curtains being drawn, just like he did with me. But she swore blind that nothing happened and that she was just visiting pals. Despite our strained relationship, I really hope that's true.

There's Nothin' Wrang!

It's been almost twenty years since my dad died. Apart from a wee baldy bit at the back of his head, he never really changed over the years, at least not physically. Once they'd moved out of Glasgow and he cut down on the booze, he couldn't do enough for us, I believe out of a sense of guilt for what we'd been through as bairns.

One day, he took a heart attack, and when he came round the doctors told him they'd discovered that he had lung cancer. He tried to put a brave face on for our sakes, saying: "Dinnae be daft, I'm not going anywhere", but though he tried to hide it, I could see him welling up.

"Aye, the doctor just says that cos he's seen yer packet of fags on the brace" (the mantelpiece) said Mum. "There's nothin' wrang wi' you". That was how she dealt with bad things; ignore them and they'll go away.

So off they went on holiday to Benidorm, their favourite destination. After recovering from a heart attack and receiving such a devastating diagnosis, a week in the Spanish sunshine with loads of cheap booze was just what Dad needed. And it was there, right in the hotel foyer, that he died. He'd suffered a massive heart attack and there was nothing that could be done to save him.

Naturally Mum was beside herself with grief, stranded in a foreign country notorious for its red tape. It was up to Pauline, the eldest in the family - and the only one of us who made it as far as university - to fly over, sort out the paperwork and bring Dad home. That was one of the worst days of my life. He may have been a boozer and a womaniser who occasionally ended up in the jail, but I loved that man to bits.

My very earliest memory is of him bringing me a pair of red wellies - I say bringing, because I'm not sure where he got them - and I remember with fondness how he would make me giggle by picking me up and tossing me over his shoulder. For him, life was for having fun and not to be taken too seriously. Mum used to describe him as 'a cross between Norman Wisdom and Frank Spencer.'

Dad had been one of a family of ten - and every one of his seven brothers had died young. I never learned why, but I guess they must have had a condition that was genetic. His dad had died in a house fire, and Dad always blamed his mother, but it's only quite recently that we found out that it was caused by one of the kids playing around with matches.

After Dad died and Mum moved to Tillicoultry, my brother Duncan would visit her every day, staying from about two in the afternoon until about seven at night, just to make sure she was okay. She'd go out to the shops in the morning to buy him a wee pie, and the two of them would spend the day together.

One day, he found her acting strangely and was so worried that he called an ambulance. In hospital, they diagnosed pneumonia, prescribed some drugs and sent her home. Then it happened again, and this time she was kept in - only to be told that she had two weeks to live.

"Dinnae be daft!" she said. "There's nothin' wrang with me! I wanna go hame."

Exactly two weeks later, she died.

To add to my distress, at about 3am I managed to fall down some hospital stairs, and I was in such pain that I thought I'd broken my hip. I was told I was going to have to be taken in, but I protested. "I cannae, I cannae," I said. "I've got to arrange my mum's funeral."

Mum's death marked my descent once again of my mental ill-health, and when Dougie died just a few weeks later, I fell apart and ended up in a psychiatric unit, diagnosed with a disturbed personality disorder.

Today, my mental health is still fragile, and I keep a wee stash of Diazepam to hand just in case I have one of my dreaded panic attacks. I'm no longer haunted by my childhood but still regretful, although I know I can't turn back time.

I don't blame Mum and Dad as they just didn't know how to parent, but I wish I'd been brought up differently. I wish I'd had parents who'd spoken about things: about the big wide world, about the reason we had to go to school. I just thought it was something to be endured, and didn't know that it was to get an education so you could make something of yourself. Apart from the wee cleaning job, the only other work I've ever done was looking after children in a community hall, which I loved, but Andrew was wee at the time and got jealous of the other bairns, so I had to give that up.

Myself and my wee Dad (RIP)

All in the Mind

Thank goodness that these days mental health issues are taken more seriously than they were when I was young.

I remember that after having my first agoraphobic episode, my first thought was to say to Derek: "Dinnae tell anybody!"

Mandy was about five at the time and Derek and I were in a cafe in Bathgate. Back then, you could still smoke indoors, so he got out his fags and lit a match. Somehow, I was mesmerised by that match, and I remember staring at it and feeling that my head had just exploded. I couldn't even see; all I knew was that I had to get out of there.

So I ran outside with Derek following me shouting: "What's wrang? What's wrang?"

All I could say was: "I'm dyin', I'm dyin!"

He somehow got me home, but all I could think of was the shame I felt. I thought I was going mad.

Derek had called the doctor, who in turn put me in touch with a psychologist. She wanted to meet me in a local library, but that in itself filled me with horror and I just couldn't do it. That marked my descent into full-on agoraphobia and resulted in Derek having to care for Mandy.

I think I'd always known that there was something wrong with me but it was to be many years before I had a proper diagnosis. At my lowest, I'd turn day into night and night into day, and, just as I'd done as a wee girl, I started conversing with God again, begging Him to help me get through it.

Some years later, I attempted to take my own life for the second time.

I'd been in a psychiatric hospital for about eight weeks, during which time the terrible emotional wounds I'd suffered when I lost Kirsten were opened up again, raw and agonisingly painful. I talked about her constantly, weeping uncontrollably, and one day it all became too much. I told staff I was going to the loo - but instead I got into the bath, still wearing all my clothes, filled it to the brim and lay back with my head fully under the water. I was away for so long that the staff came looking for me, and ended up forcing the bathroom door open and pulling me out. Mixed with the regret that once again I was still alive was the terrible guilt I felt and I'll never forget Andrew crying: "Mum, I need you, I need you."

It was relatively recently - just about seven years ago - that I finally got a proper diagnosis, and even then it didn't happen without trauma.

I had been referred to a psychologist in Dumfries, and at one point during the consultation I overheard her saying: "She's not suffering from depression." Well, I lost the plot. All those years of feeling so low I wanted to die; of feeling so down that I was literally incapable of moving until Dougie chucked those bloody purple hearts down my throat ... and I wasn't suffering from depression? What kind of a quack was this woman?

I ran out of the hospital, down through the town and jumped into the River Nith, sparking an emergency with the local police.

Having dragged me out of the water and dried me out, they took me back to hospital, where the psychologist said calmly: "You didn't let me finish."

She went on to tell me that I was suffering from emotional disturbed personality disorder, which manifests itself in intense emotions that fluctuate wildly and is most commonly caused by childhood instability or distress, abuse and traumatic life events. Well, I ticked all those boxes and it was a relief to be able to put a name to my condition at long last.

I was prescribed Olanzapine, an anti-psychotic drug that made me put on weight at such an alarming rate that, stupidly, I stopped taking it. That led to horrific withdrawal symptoms and I remember one day sitting naked in a friend's house, rocking back and forth and saying: "I cannae sit at peace!"

I've had bad reactions to quite a few drugs but now I think I'm on a course of medication that keeps me stable.

*Andrew Duncan Clinic at The Royal Edinburgh Hospital where I have
spent some time for mental health problems*

*Royal Edinburgh Hospital, I was admitted to The Ritson Clinic for
alcohol problems*

Midpark Psychiatric Hospital in Dumfries

Midpark Hospital where I have spent some time for mental health issues

True Friends

I really don't know where I'd be without my friends - in particular Gary, who's now my carer and my rock. We did start our relationship on a romantic basis, but it's developed over the years into something far stronger; a deep and abiding friendship without all the complications!

I first met him at the Cavendish Club in Edinburgh and we clicked immediately. He was the drummer in a well-known 70s band and was different from any man I'd ever known. He told me his marriage was on its last legs, and as I had split from Dougie and was living with a friend, my relationship was over too.

Gary is English, and I remember when I first introduced him to my parents, Mum said drily: "We dinnae like the English, do we Wullie?"

But that was just their Glaswegian humour, and they soon grew to like and respect him.

Gary and I got married in a pretty village just outside Perth; I wore a gorgeous white gown that made me feel like Cinderella and it was a magical day, complete with outside catering and flowing champagne - a world away from my first wedding, the £11 dress and dodgy accordionist. We had two receptions - the first in the village and the second in Whitburn, where we stayed overnight in a hotel. The day had been beautiful, but the next morning I had a massive panic attack.

"I cannae be married to you!" I said to Gary.

"You need to take your ring back; I dinnae like this feeling!

Can we just go back to being boyfriend and girlfriend?"

I just had an overwhelming feeling of being trapped, probably because of my previous experiences, and felt overwhelmed with fear at the prospect of being committed to this man. From then, the nature of our relationship shifted: he grew up but I didn't. In his fifties, he became increasingly crabbit; I used to tell him he was turning into Victor Meldrew. If there's such a thing as a male menopause, he has all the symptoms! But despite his grumpiness, he is without doubt the kindest man I've ever known, a true gentleman who gave me encouragement instead of constant criticism, who took me on my first-ever holiday and who would do anything for me. We were officially married for seven years before finally getting divorced, having settled into a comfortable relationship as best friends. We've seen each other every single day for almost twenty-five years and care for each other deeply.

Then there was Wilma, who I met through a mutual friend in Edinburgh, and right from the start, we couldn't stop blethering. She was a massive support to me when I was going through my troubles with Dougie; in fact, not long after we met and after a particularly savage beating, I turned up on her doorstep with all my worldly goods in a couple of carrier bags. "I hardly ken ye, and here you are, turning up at ma door wi' yer bloody bags!" she said. But of course she took me in, and remained a source of comfort throughout the whole sad saga with Kirsten.

Although Wilma was always in my thoughts, it was only recently that I decided to phone her to see how she was. Her husband answered, telling me she couldn't come to the phone right now. In the morning, I discovered why. That night, Wilma passed away, and I was consumed with guilt. I hadn't even known she was ill, and I hadn't been there for her, as she had always been there for me.

In an effort to make amends - and salve my conscience - I helped Wilma's dad, who had had a cancer diagnosis. But I know that wasn't enough. Rest in peace Wilma, my dear friend.

I do try to go out occasionally as I know it's good for me, and when I do it's invariably with my friends Morag and Cathy.

Cathy would call herself 'the bank manager', as when I was skint I'd say: "Any chance o' a wee tap, Cathy?" And she'd say: "How much, Mia? I'll put it in yer account."

Morag, too, is generous to me. If she comes into some extra cash, she'll say: "Come on Mia, let's go oot and I'll treat you to a wee lippy!" Sometimes, she's even booked us a limo so that we can hit the clubs of Edinburgh in style.

Morag is a bit too generous with the booze though and tries to get you pissed even before you've left the house. I've learned from experience that once you've had issues with alcohol - and recovered - that you can never drink in the same way again. So when Morag gives me a huge vodka, I wait until she's not looking, then tip it into the sink and top up my glass with lemonade. I confess to needing a couple of small drinks before I go out, otherwise I'd be rigid with fear, although I know my pals are looking out for me. Once out, I'll nurse a half of lager all night and if I have to go to the loo, I'll never return to the same drink as the thought of it being spiked fills me with absolute terror.

I do enjoy a wee night out with my pals, and I'm grateful to them for their understanding and encouragement because they know I can't plan anything in advance. I just don't know how I'm going to feel, and I hate letting people down.

Life has been tough. I have regrets. I've made mistakes. But I've survived.

My dear friend Gary often says to me: "You're stronger than you think you are."

A weekend away with Kathy and friends

A weekend away with friends where we met Paul Shane from Hi De Hi

My 40th Birthday present

Myself and one of my Brothers

The day of my wedding to Gary in our house

Lessons Learned

My last relationship was relatively recently, with a man I met in the local pub - on the face of it a real charmer, although to begin with I didn't fancy him that much as he had a wee paunch and not much hair. But when he turned up on his Harley Davidson the next day, I was smitten. He told me he and his wife were living separate lives, that she was away on holiday and he was free as a bird. The way he talked to me made me feel special; he ticked all my boxes, but somewhere in the back of my mind a tiny warning bell was sounding which, of course, I chose to ignore. We were even planning a cruise together - until one morning, as we lay in bed, I got a text from a friend.

'Mia, get out of there, he's a cheating scumbag!' it read.

I shot out of bed; shouted, bawled and called him for everything, then got a taxi home. I couldn't get out of there quickly enough.

It turned out that he wasn't separated at all - his wife had died very shortly before we met, but he'd decided that was none of my business. Not only that, but he'd also been seeing another woman. We'd been together for eight months but he refused to update his status on Facebook to 'in a relationship', which did make me suspicious, but, once again, I chose to ignore my doubts.

I've made many mistakes over the years, but at times my self-esteem has been so low and my mental health so poor that I simply didn't recognise the situations that I was getting myself into. However, I have learned lessons and I hope my experiences will help others too. Often women don't realise that they're being controlled until it's too late; the man will be all over them at first, showering them with love and making them feel they can't live without them. Then they start delivering subtle but cruel little barbs, especially if you're going out without them ... ... *'That dress is a bit short, isn't it?' 'That outfit makes you look fat? 'Why are you wearing make- up?'*

Dougie would tell me I was a fat bitch, then buy me a massive bar of chocolate; he'd mock my lack of reading and writing skills but took the piss out of me when I signed up for evening classes to try to improve them. Little by little, he wore me down until my confidence was at rock bottom. So my advice to others is to be wary if he's just too smothering; all too often that's an early warning sign that he's a control freak. Domestic abuse isn't just physical, and in fact using coercive and controlling behaviour is now a criminal offence.

Now that I'm a grandmother, I'm heartened that society is so much more sensitive to the signs that a child has been sexually abused. It was only during one of my many stays in hospital that staff were alerted to the fact that I'd been abused - and quite possibly raped - because of the redness 'down below'. Otherwise, it would have gone unnoticed. My parents were too wrapped up in their own lives to notice that I'd become withdrawn and anxious, and of course my wee mum just wouldn't accept that a drinking pal of Dad's would do something so vile. In the end, he essentially got away with it as he died before any criminal charges could be brought against him, but I'll never forget the feelings of guilt, shame and helplessness that no child should ever have to endure.

When I look back at my life, I'm reminded of a particularly dramatic soap opera. It's been a life of abuse, tragedy and deprivation - but with Gary by my side, I try to stay positive.

And despite all I've been through, I'd love to find love again, this time with a man who I can trust implicitly and who loves me for who I am.

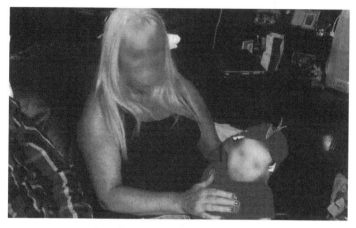

Myself and one of my Grandchildren

Printed in Great Britain
by Amazon

45407594R00042